FROM SEA to SHINING SEA

MISSOURI

MARY ELLEN LAGO

Consultants

MELISSA N. MATUSEVICH, PH.D.

Curriculum and Instruction Specialist
Blacksburg, Virginia

VICKY BAKER

Librarian
Mid-Continent Public Library
Lee's Summit, Missouri

CHILDREN'S PRESS®
A DIVISION OF SCHOLASTIC INC.

New York · Toronto · London · Auckland · Sydney · Mexico City
New Delhi · Hong Kong · Danbury, Connecticut

Missouri is in the midwestern United States. It is bordered by Illinois, Kentucky, Tennessee, Arkansas, Oklahoma, Kansas, Nebraska, and Iowa.

The photograph on the front cover shows a view of the Mississippi River and the Gateway Arch in St. Louis.

Project Editor: Meredith DeSousa
Art Director: Marie O'Neill
Photo Researcher: Marybeth Kavanagh
Design: Robin West, Ox and Company, Inc.
Page 6 map and recipe art: Susan Hunt Yule
All other maps: XNR Productions, Inc.

Library of Congress Cataloging-in-Publication Data

Lago, Mary Ellen.
  Missouri / Mary Ellen Lago.
    p. cm. — (From sea to shining sea)
Summary: Takes the reader on a tour of the state once called the "Gateway to the West,"
emphasizing its geography, history, government, and culture.
Includes bibliographical references and index.
  ISBN 0-516-22390-9
  Missouri—Juvenile literature. [1. Missouri.] I. Title. II. Series.
  F466.3 .L34 2003
  977.8—dc21   2002009026

TABLE of CONTENTS

CHAPTER ONE

INTRODUCING THE SHOW ME STATE

A trio of cyclists enjoy the outdoors near Kansas City.

The slogan of Graham, Missouri, "A Pioneer Town with the Space Age Spirit," describes the state as well. Missouri grew up as a pioneer settlement. Brave explorers, clever fur traders, and determined pioneers came to Missouri. Many pioneers passed through Missouri on their way to the western frontier. So many people passed through that the state became known as the "Gateway to the West."

If traveling by horse, pioneers followed the famous Santa Fe or Oregon trails that began in Independence, Missouri. If traveling by boat, which was faster and easier, pioneers could choose one of two great rivers: the Missouri River or the Mississippi River. In fact, *Missouri* is a Native American word that means "people in big canoes." The pioneers who decided to stay had beautiful mountains, prairies, and rich soil to settle. Missouri promised people a fine life.

Today, Missouri still promises a fine life in the beautiful countryside or in modern cities with the "Space Age Spirit." Missouri is home to manufacturers of automobiles, jet airplanes, medicines, and chemicals. With more than five and a half million people calling Missouri home, the "Show Me State" has the seventeenth largest population of all the states in the country.

Missouri got its nickname, the "Show Me State," in 1899. Missouri Congressman Willard Duncan Vandiver said he didn't like fancy speeches and words. He once said, "I'm from Missouri and you've got to show me." Today Missouri has plenty to show:

* Towboats pushing barges on the Mississippi River
* The great St. Louis Gateway Arch
* The music and arts of the Ozarks
* The Pony Express Museum
* Kansas City, "the City of Fountains"
* The Mark Twain National Forest

Missouri is filled with history and tradition. It has big cities and tall mountains. It has people of many nationalities and backgrounds. Turn the page to discover the very special state of Missouri.

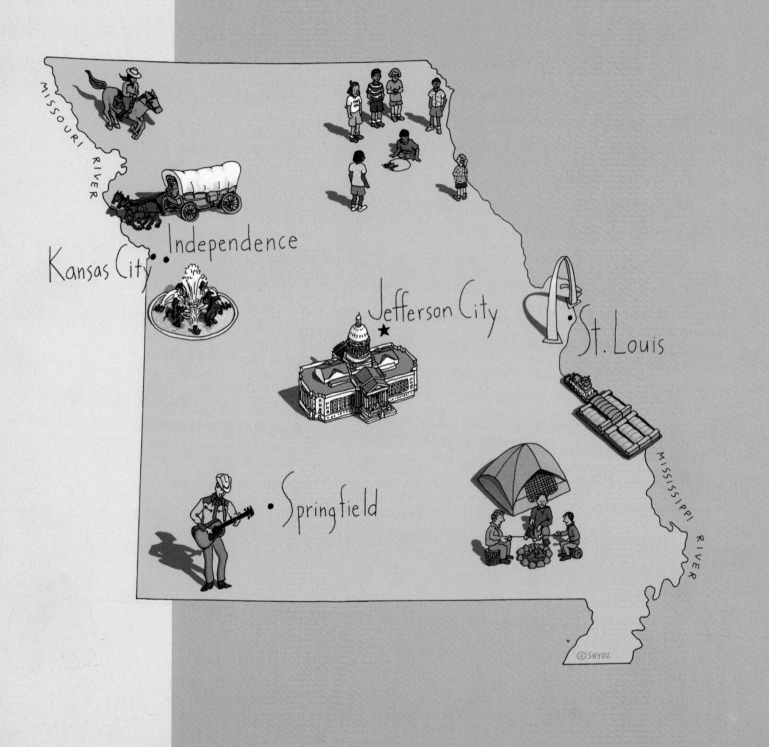

Kansas City

Independence

Jefferson City

St. Louis

Springfield

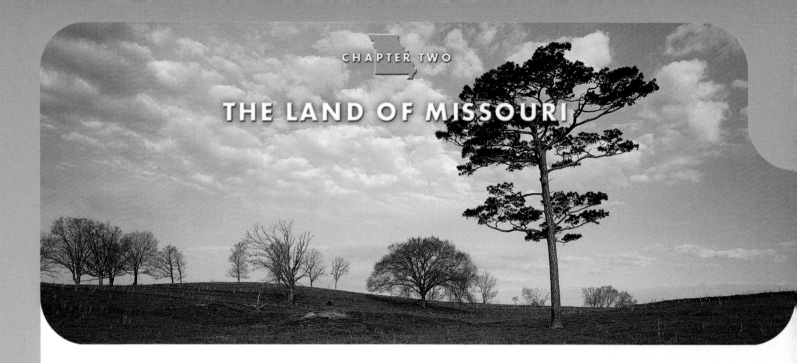

CHAPTER TWO

THE LAND OF MISSOURI

Missouri is located in the middle of the United States, in an area called the Midwest. The Midwest is a group of ten states in the north central part of the country. Missouri is the twenty-first largest state in the country, with 69,709 square miles (180,545 square kilometers) of land and water.

Eight states surround Missouri. Iowa is to the north and Arkansas is to the south. Oklahoma, Kansas, and Nebraska are Missouri's neighbors to the west. Tennessee, Illinois, and Kentucky are its neighbors to the east. Because it is surrounded by so many states, Missouri has been called one of the most neighborly states in the country.

Residents and visitors enjoy exploring Missouri's quiet beauty.

HOW THE LAND WAS FORMED

The rock that sits under Missouri's soil today was once boiling lava from volcanoes that exploded billions of years ago. The lava shot up, covered

FIND OUT MORE

Only one other state has as many neighbors as Missouri. What state is it? Who are its neighbors?

the ground, and then cooled, forming a rocky layer. Pressure from underneath pushed up the rocky layer to form the Ozark and St. Francois mountains.

Both the Ozark and St. Francois mountains differ from other mountains. Most mountains run north to south. The Ozark and St. Francois mountains run east to west.

The highest point in Missouri is Taum Sauk Mountain, at 1,772 feet (540 meters) above sea level. Taum Sauk is part of the St. Francois Mountains. Even though the ocean covered Missouri for a long time, Taum Sauk was never underwater. It is one of the few high points in the world that was never under oceans or glaciers.

A walk to the top of Taum Sauk offers visitors a beautiful view of the St. Francois Mountains.

After millions of years, the ocean moved back and the Ice Age began. When the earth cooled, the water turned to ice, shrinking the ocean. Temperatures continued to drop, and snow fell. The snow packed tighter and tighter until it turned into glaciers that were hundreds of feet thick. Two of these glaciers moved down from the north and covered Missouri all the way to the Missouri River.

Like a giant broom, the glaciers pushed rocks, sand, and gravel forward. When the warm air returned, the ice melted. The dirt that was left behind became Missouri's rich farmland and rolling hills. Rotting animal carcasses and plants in the soil made it richer and gave it a black color. This black dirt is called *till*.

GEOGRAPHIC AREAS

There are four geographic areas in Missouri: The Dissected Till Plains, the Osage Plains, the Ozark Plateau, and the Mississippi Alluvial Plain.

The Dissected Till Plains

Geologists (scientists who study the land) call the northern part of Missouri the Dissected Till Plains. A *plain* is a large flat piece of land. *Dissected* means the land has been divided by rivers into hills. The Dissected Till Plains is a mostly flat area of land with small, gentle hills and rich soil.

Stretching from the Iowa border to the Missouri River, this area also has many streams and rivers flowing through it. Farmers have always

A farmer near St. Joseph gets the ground ready for spring planting.

found these grassy plains productive for farming. Today, corn, soybeans, and wheat are grown in this area.

The Osage Plains

South of the Missouri River and north of the Osage River in west central Missouri is the Osage Plains. This area differs from the Dissected Till Plains because it is flatter, the soil is not as rich, and there are fewer streams and rivers.

Great herds of buffalo once grazed on the prairie grass that grows in this region, which is sometimes called the Old Plains. Today the Old

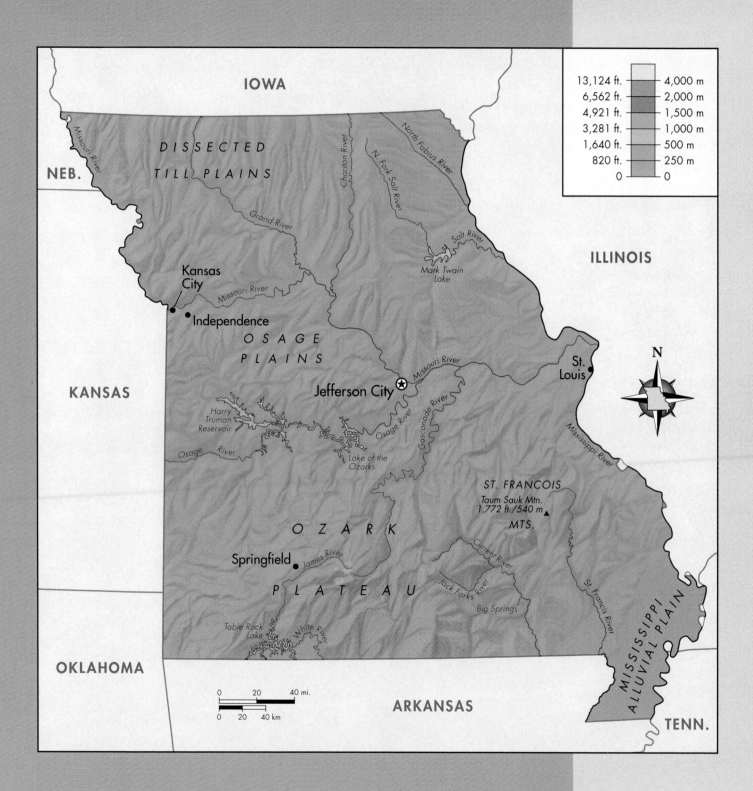

IOWA

NEB.

KANSAS

OKLAHOMA

ILLINOIS

TENN.

ARKANSAS

13,124 ft.	4,000 m
6,562 ft.	2,000 m
4,921 ft.	1,500 m
3,281 ft.	1,000 m
1,640 ft.	500 m
820 ft.	250 m
0	0

N

DISSECTED TILL PLAINS

Missouri River

Grand River

Chariton River

N. Fork Salt River

North Fabius River

Salt River

Mark Twain Lake

Kansas City

Independence

Missouri River

OSAGE PLAINS

Jefferson City

Missouri River

St. Louis

Harry Truman Reservoir

Osage River

Lake of the Ozarks

Osage River

Gasconade River

Mississippi River

ST. FRANCOIS
Taum Sauk Mtn.
1,772 ft./540 m ▲
MTS.

OZARK

Springfield

James River

Current River

Jacks Forks River

Big Springs

St. Francis River

PLATEAU

Table Rock Lake

White River

MISSISSIPPI ALLUVIAL PLAIN

0   20   40 mi.
0   20   40 km

11

The Ozark Plateau is a scenic area filled with mountains, forests, lakes, and rivers. Jack Forks River is pictured here.

Plains is used for growing oats and corn and for raising beef and dairy cattle.

The Ozark Plateau

The Ozark Plateau is the largest geographic area in Missouri. It covers the southern half of Missouri except for the southeastern corner. There are clear rivers and lakes as well as many beautiful caves in this region.

The Ozark Plateau has steep limestone mountains covered with forests. Millions of acres in these parts were once thought of as dead after

people cut down too many trees. Care and management have made the forests healthy again. Today the Ozark Plateau has some of the wildest natural growth in the Midwest.

Rivers and streams in this area have worn away the surface of the land, creating many canyons and valleys. This is the roughest and most uneven area in Missouri, but it is a good place for gardens and for vacationing near the lakes and rivers.

FIND OUT MORE

Missouri has more than five thousand caves and many streams. Some of Missouri's streams begin in caves. What do you think the continuous flow of water over thousands of years has done to the caves?

Bald cypress trees grow in a Missouri swamp near Mark Twain National Forest.

The Mississippi Alluvial Plain

In the southeastern corner of Missouri is the smallest geographic area, the Mississippi Alluvial Plain. *Alluvial* means it was made by mud from flowing water. The Alluvial Plain in Missouri was made by mud from the Mississippi River. Missouri's "boot heel" is also in this area. This swampy area sticks out from the bottom of the state, and is shaped like a boot heel. The Alluvial Plain once swarmed with mosquitoes. In 1905, the Little River Drainage District drained the area with man-made canals (big ditches) to make it into useful farmland. Rice, cotton, and soybeans are some of the crops grown in this area today.

RIVERS AND LAKES

The muddiest water in Missouri comes from the Missouri River. The river flows 2,540 miles (4,090 kilometers) beginning in the Rocky Mountains in southeastern Montana. Flowing south it becomes Missouri's western border until it reaches Kansas City. At Kansas City, the Missouri turns east and enters the state. It continues to flow east to just north of St. Louis, where it joins the Mississippi River. Along the way it picks up mud and dirt from the bottom and sides of the river. The water becomes so thick and syrupy that it earned the nickname "Big Muddy." Early pioneers joked that "the Big Muddy's too thick to drink and too thin to plow."

The Missouri and Mississippi rivers converge near St. Louis.

14

When the muddy Missouri spills into the lighter waters of the great Mississippi River, they look like two different rivers. Finally, the waters mix and the Mississippi flows on, forever changed by the Missouri's mud.

The mighty Mississippi starts at Lake Itasca in northwestern Minnesota. It flows south to the Gulf of Mexico for 2,350 miles (3,782 km). Along the way, it forms the entire eastern border of the state of Missouri.

There are many other rivers in Missouri. The Osage River begins in Kansas and flows east through Missouri for about 300 miles (483 km). It empties into the Missouri River at Jefferson City. In the 1800s, the Osage River was an important means of transportation. Pioneers and settlers depended on it to receive supplies. Today, vacationers use the Osage River for fishing and water sports.

The Current and Jack Forks rivers are in southeastern Missouri. These rivers have not changed since Native Americans slept on their banks. Both the Current and Jack Forks rivers are known for their quick flowing currents and clear water. Vacationers ride the rivers on boats, rafts, and floats through thick forests. On the way, they enjoy the wildlife and beautiful natural growth that surround them.

In northern Missouri, the Grand River flows from its source in southwestern Iowa. Continuing south through Missouri, the Grand joins the Missouri River near Brunswick. In pioneer days, the Grand was not large enough or deep enough for steamboat travel. In fact, the town of Bedford,

Two men paddle down the Meramec River in central Missouri.

Missouri, was named for the steamboat *Bedford*. The *Bedford* struck a log and was damaged beyond repair because of low water in the Grand River. Today the Grand flows through farm country and is used for fishing.

In northeastern Missouri, the Salt and Fabius rivers flow southeast into the Mississippi. Both rivers are used today for fishing. The Fabius is said to have some of the best catfish around.

With all these rivers, Missourians are concerned about spring floods. Melting snow and spring rains can cause the rivers to overflow. To hold back the water, Missourians built dams. When the dam's gates close, the water stops, and when they are open the water flows through. Dams can also be built to generate power. To do this, water is carefully controlled and released through turbines, or engines, that create electricity.

Some of these dams created lakes called reservoirs. A reservoir is a place where water is stored. When the Bagnell Dam was built across the Osage River in 1931, it backed up the water. The water filled the surrounding canyons and valleys, creating the famous octopus-shaped Lake of the Ozarks.

The Harry Truman Dam built on the Osage River created the Harry Truman Reservoir in west central Missouri. The reservoir is part of a state park where you can enjoy swimming, fishing, horseback riding, camping, and hiking.

Mark Twain Lake is in northeast Missouri on the Salt River. Table Rock Lake is on the White River in southwestern Missouri. Both lakes were created by dams.

Table Rock Lake Dam was built in 1958. The lake itself offers a variety of recreational activities.

NATURAL SPRINGS

Missouri is well-known for its many natural springs. A spring is a small stream of water flowing naturally from the earth. The springs might have been created by cracks

FIND OUT MORE

In 1929, the Union Electric Light and Power Company of St. Louis hired 10,000 men to build the Bagnell Dam. At that time, it was the biggest construction project in the nation. Why would a light and power company spend so much money to build a dam?

Springs are found throughout the Ozarks, providing some of the cleanest water on earth.

in the limestone. These cracks may have been created by a fault line in southeastern Missouri. A fault line is a break in the rock deep under the soil. The spring's water bubbles up from the crack.

Springs have always been interesting and exciting. Springs were once thought to be helpful for sick people, who would travel for miles to swim in or drink from the spring water in hopes that it would cure them.

In southeastern Missouri near Van Buren, Big Springs is part of the Ozark National Scenic Riverways. Many people visit this national park. Big Springs is one of the largest springs in the world. It puts out about 846 million gallons (3.2 billion liters) of water every day.

CLIMATE

All of Missouri shares the same type of weather. Summer temperatures average about 78° Fahrenheit (26° Celsius), although a much wider range of temperatures is possible. The hottest recorded temperature was on July 15, 1936, when it rose to 118° F (48° C) in Clinton. During winter months it gets cold enough to snow, dropping to about 30° F (–1° C). The coldest recorded temperature in Missouri was on February 13, 1905, when it dropped to –40° F (–40° C) in Warsaw.

Storm clouds often roll in from the west, so Missourians are used to lots of rain, thunderstorms, and, sometimes, deadly tornadoes. A tornado is a fast-turning, funnel-shaped whirlwind that touches the ground, destroying anything in its path. On March 18, 1925, one of the worst tornadoes in the United States began near Ellington in southeastern

The flat land in Missouri and other Midwestern states contributes to the formation of tornadoes.

Missouri. Trees were snapped in two, farms were destroyed, and many people were killed as the tornado traveled more than 100 miles (161 km) in three and a half hours.

Most of Missouri's rain comes in gentle rainstorms. In the boot heel, it rains about 50 inches (127 cm) per year. Northern Missouri is drier, with an average rainfall of 32 inches (81 cm) yearly. During the cold winter months, it snows about 20 inches (51 cm) per year.

The shaking of earthquakes is also part of life in Missouri. The most powerful earthquake recorded in North America occurred on December 16, 1811, in New Madrid. People in this southeastern Missouri town were woken up by "the rocking of their cabins, the cracking of timbers, the clatter of breaking dishes and tumbling furniture," according to the National Earthquake Information Center. The earthquake caused huge waves on the Mississippi River and even caused the river to flow backward. There are still earthquakes in Missouri today, but none as large as the one in 1811.

CHAPTER THREE

MISSOURI THROUGH HISTORY

About ten thousand years ago, the first people of the land we now call Missouri lived among the green valleys and flowing rivers. They were called the Bluff Dwellers. They lived in caves and hunted black bears and giant beavers. Making canoes, planting crops, and eating berries and fish were also part of their daily lives. For no known reason, the Bluff Dwellers disappeared around 7000 B.C.

Long after the Bluff Dwellers, the Mound Builders began to inhabit the area in A.D. 700. These Native Americans were called Mound Builders because they built large mounds of dirt slowly, step-by-step, one basket load at a time. Some mounds were small round "temple mounds" where bones and jewelry were buried. Others were flat on top where structures once

In the late 1800s, St. Louis was a major port on the Mississippi River.

FIND OUT MORE

In 1839, Dr. Albert Koch, a scientist who studied fossils, uncovered the complete skeleton of a mastodon near Kimmswick, Missouri. Mastodons lived thousands of years ago. They looked like elephants with huge tusks. Dr. Koch displayed the mastodon skeleton in his St. Louis museum. Today, when scientists uncover ancient bones, what do they do with them? How do they care for them?

The Mound Builders created pottery with painted designs.

stood. The Mound Builders lived along the banks of the Mississippi River. They grew crops and traded with tribes from other areas. In the 1500s, the Mound Builders also mysteriously disappeared.

During the 1600s, other Native American tribes moved to what would later become Missouri. They came from the eastern United States where white settlers were taking over the land. The Sauk and Fox lived north of the Missouri River. The women grew corn in summer and the men hunted in winter. Several families lived together in large bark-covered homes. The Missouri tribe lived in the eastern and central areas of present-day Missouri. They lived in earth-covered houses, hunted buffalo, and farmed the land.

EXTRA! EXTRA!

Some of the mounds made by the Mound Builders can still be seen in Missouri today. The largest is near Caruthersville. At 400 feet (122 m) long and 250 feet (76 m) wide, it is longer than a football field and almost as wide. It stands 35 feet (11 m) high. No one is sure what it was used for, but it may have had a temple on it.

The Sauk and Fox Indians sometimes met in Missouri.

The Osage tribe lived in the southern and western areas of Missouri along the Osage River. They were the largest tribe in the area. The men were known to be over 6 feet (2 m) tall, and the women wore perfume made from plants. Hunting bear and beaver was part of their daily lives. The Osage also planted crops such as corn, beans, and pumpkins.

EUROPEAN EXPLORERS

In 1673, the Osage met two European explorers, Louis Joliet and Father Jacques Marquette. These Frenchmen came from Canada to explore the Mississippi River, hoping to find a route to the Pacific Ocean. They did not find a way to the Pacific, but they did find the mouth of the Missouri River. The Osage called the men *I-shta-hi*, which means "squint

Jacques Marquette and Louis Joliet sailed down the Mississippi River in search of a route to the Pacific Ocean.

eyes." Because the explorers traveled from sunup to sundown, their faces were chapped from the sun and they squinted.

In 1682, an explorer named René-Robert Cavelier, Sieur de La Salle, put a French flag into the Mississippi's mud and claimed all the land the river touched for King Louis XIV of France. He called this region Louisiana, and it included present-day Missouri.

More Frenchmen came to this new land to hunt and trade furs. The French wanted to trade beaver furs with the Osage because the Osage were skilled beaver trappers. The beaver furs could then be sold in Europe, where they were used to make hats and capes.

By 1750, the Osage were working with Frenchman Pierre Laclede of New Orleans. He had scouted the land and found a place for his headquarters. Laclede sent his thirteen-year-old stepson, René Auguste Chouteau, and a crew of men to build a fur trading post. The trading post, called Laclede's Landing, was just a few small buildings where the Osage traded furs with the Europeans. Laclede's Landing was the beginning of present-day St. Louis.

Meanwhile, more Frenchmen rushed to Osage lands to search for silver. Lead had been found there, and it was believed that where there was lead, there was silver. Working for the French-owned Company of the West, Philip Renault arrived in 1720. He brought the first African slaves to Missouri. The slaves were kidnapped from their homes in Africa and forced to work in the mines. They were treated like property, and were bought and sold at marketplaces. If slaves tried to leave they could be beaten or killed. Renault never found silver, but he found iron in southeastern Missouri at Potosi. Renault stayed and made his slaves work the mines until 1744.

Philip Renault smelted (melted) iron ore, then transported it to Illinois, where it could be sold.

Chief Pawhuska (? – 1808), also called Cheveau Blanc or Chief White Hair, was chief of the Osage in the late 1700s and early 1800s. Chief Pawhuska wanted his people to live peacefully with the European settlers. In 1804, he traveled to Washington, D.C. to meet with President Thomas Jefferson. In Washington he stated that his main concern was for his people. He wanted to "reunite the Osage people as a tribe." During the one hundred years after his death in 1808, other Osage leaders named themselves White Hair to honor this great leader.

THE LOUISIANA PURCHASE

In the mid-1700s, fur traders from both England and Spain were in the areas surrounding the Louisiana Territory. In 1762, France made a treaty with Spain. The treaty gave Louisiana, including present-day Missouri, to Spain. Jealousy grew between old French fur traders and new Spanish fur traders. Both the French and Spanish wanted the Osage to trade with them.

The Osage did not like seeing the men argue. Osage Chief Big Soldier told the Europeans, "You are surrounded by slaves. Everything about you is in chains, and you are in chains yourselves." He told them that if he acted the way they did, "I fear, I too, should become a slave."

However, Spanish and French traders continued to fight about fur trading with the Osage. This caused the Osage tribe to divide in 1796. Some of the tribe stayed in the village with Chief Pawhuska. Others moved north and started a new village. By 1800, the tribes were unhappy, divided, and confused.

In 1800, Spain lost a war with France and gave Louisiana back to France. However, France had been fighting wars for many years and needed money. In 1803, France sold the Louisiana Territory, including

French and U.S. officials negotiated the terms for the Louisiana Purchase.

Lewis and Clark kept a diary to record information about the things they saw.

present-day Missouri, to the United States for $15 million. This was called the Louisiana Purchase.

United States President Thomas Jefferson wanted to explore the new territory he had bought. To do this, he selected Meriwether Lewis and William Clark to be in charge of an expedition. Jefferson sent them on a "quest of knowledge," to explore the land of Louisiana. In 1804, Lewis and Clark began their journey in St. Louis and started up the Missouri River. They made it all the way to the Pacific Ocean and returned to St. Louis more than two years later with maps, plants, and information about the new land.

THE PIONEERS

When Lewis and Clark returned from their journey, they described rich prairies and told about all the animals and plants they saw. They made detailed maps of the land and waterways. Many people were excited by their reports and wanted to travel to the new territory. Pioneers and settlers poured into the area.

On June 4, 1812, Missouri became a territory of the United States. An 1820 guidebook bragged, "There is no part of the western country that holds out greater advantages to the new settler than the Missouri Territory." Pioneers cleared the land for farms and built log cabins. They made furniture, fiddles, and cloth. When newcomers settled in the area, the neighbors helped to build their home. In one day, they could build a house and still have time to celebrate that night.

Some pioneers only passed through Missouri on their way west. Missouri was the last stop for supplies before heading into the unknown frontier. From St. Joseph, there were two trails for wagon trains. The

Santa Fe Trail, started in 1821, went south for about 900 miles (1,448 km) to Santa Fe in present-day New Mexico. The Oregon Trail started in 1841 and went north for about 2,000 miles (3,219 km) to present-day Oregon.

The first railroad west of the Mississippi and in Missouri began in 1852 in St. Louis. Only 5 miles (8 km) long at the time, it eventually went across the state to Kansas City. The King's Highway, running from St. Louis to southeast Missouri, became the first legal road in Missouri. Other roads at the time were made with wooden planks.

As Missouri's population increased, Native Americans were forced to move farther west. In 1836, the last of the Native Americans' land was signed over to the United States in a treaty called the Platte Purchase.

After that, Native Americans had no more land claims in Missouri. They moved into the Indian Territory in present-day Kansas and Nebraska.

ACCEPTANCE INTO THE UNION

Many of Missouri's settlers were farmers who owned slaves. In 1819, Missouri had more than 10,000 slaves. Throughout the United States, there were mixed feelings about slavery. Many Northerners felt it was wrong and that it should be abolished, or ended. In the South, however, farmers needed workers for their farms. Southerners wanted each state to make its own laws about slavery. They didn't want to be told they couldn't have slaves.

In 1817, the people of Missouri asked the United States Congress (the country's law-makers) if they could become a state. Northerners in Congress refused because Missouri would have to be admitted as a slave state. If this were allowed, there would be more slave states than free states (states without slavery). Then, the southern states would have more power and could make the country's laws about slavery.

EXTRA! EXTRA!

Some settlers were not welcomed in Missouri. The Mormons, also known as members of the Church of Jesus Christ of Latter-day Saints, settled in Independence in 1831. The Mormons were against slavery, which made them unpopular with Missouri farmers. Missourians began attacking the Mormons in what became known as the Mormon Wars. The fighting became so bad that Missouri governor Lilburn W. Boggs ordered the Mormons to leave Missouri in 1838. Most had left by the following year, settling first in Illinois and then Utah.

For several years, Northerners and Southerners argued about Missouri becoming a state. Finally, in 1820, Congress created the Missouri Compromise. It allowed Missouri to be admitted as a slave state, and the northern state of Maine to be admitted as a free state. This gave equal representation to both North and South. On August 10, 1821, Missouri became the twenty-fourth state. With a population of 66,586, Missourians elected Alexander McNair as the state's first governor.

Alexander McNair was the first elected governor of Missouri.

THE CIVIL WAR

The Missouri Compromise solved the first crisis over slavery. However, it wasn't long before a new conflict arose. In 1846, a slave named Dred Scott went to a St. Louis court and demanded his freedom. Previously, Scott had traveled and lived in free states with his owner. Because he had once lived on free land, Scott thought he should be free.

It took more than ten years before the case finally went to the United States Supreme Court. In 1857, the Court refused to grant Scott his freedom. The Court said that, because Scott was a slave, he was not a United States citizen and did not have the right to file a lawsuit in a United States court. This

WHAT'S IN A NAME?

Some place names in Missouri have interesting origins.

Name	Comes From or Means
St. Louis	Named after King Louis XIV of France
Ozark	French word *auxarks*, meaning "territory of Arkansas Indians"
Missouri	Fox Indian word meaning "big canoe people"
Mississippi River	Ojibwe words *missi sipi* meaning "great water"
Osage	Mispronunciation of Native American "Wazhazhe" tribe

was a very important case because it kept slavery legal and also refused African-Americans their citizenship.

When this happened, North and South became even more divided. In 1860, the southern states decided to leave the United States to start their own nation. It was called the Confederate States of America. Within a few months, eleven southern states joined the Confederacy.

The United States government refused to accept the Confederacy as a separate nation. The northern states chose to fight to keep the country together. This fight was called the Civil War (1861–1865).

Missouri stayed with the United States, but not all of its citizens agreed. Some sided with the Union, while others sided with the Confederacy. During the Civil War, Missouri became a bloody battlefield. There were more than 1,100 battles on Missouri soil. On January 11, 1865, Missouri became the first state to free its slaves. On April 9, the war ended when the Confederate Army surrendered to the Union Army.

Dred Scott spent eleven years in court fighting for his freedom.

During the Civil War, many Missourians who supported slavery crossed over the border into Kansas.

32

RECONSTRUCTION

By the end of the Civil War, more than 114,000 slaves in Missouri were free. Many moved to the North where they were more welcome and there were more jobs. Some stayed and continued to work for their former owners. Others looked for jobs with the skills they knew. They became maids, cooks, and farmhands. In 1870, two in every three African-Americans in Missouri were farmers. Some free slaves opened businesses. In Kansas City, Mrs. Alphia Smith Minor opened the first ready-made dress shop in the city.

Although African-Americans were free, times were not easy for them. They were not allowed to join whites in schools, hotels, or restaurants. In Missouri, a law was passed for separate schools for the freed slaves, but whites voted against spending money on these schools. In 1870, only a small number of African-American children were in school.

As the newly freed slaves struggled to rebuild their lives, Missourians were rebuilding their state. Railroads, highways, bridges, and public buildings destroyed during the war needed to be fixed. Missourians worked hard to make these repairs.

FAMOUS FIRSTS

The Missouri School for the Blind in St. Louis was the first in the United States to use Braille (a system of writing or printing for use by the blind) in 1859.

In St. Louis, Captain Berry became the first person to jump successfully from a moving airplane in 1912. He used a hot-air balloon for a parachute.

C. H. Laessig started the world's first gasoline station in St. Louis in 1905. The gas, which previously had to be bought in cans at grocery stores, was pumped through a garden hose.

St. Louis was the site of the first automobile accident in 1895. Even though there were only four gasoline cars in the United States, two crashed in St. Louis, injuring both drivers.

The first daylight bank robbery in the United States took place in Liberty, Missouri. On February 13, 1866, robbers stole more than $60,000 from the Clay County Savings Bank and Loan Association. It is believed that Jesse James was the leader of the bandits.

The 250-foot (76-m) Ferris wheel at the St. Louis World's Fair was the largest at the time.

In 1904, proud Missourians invited the world to visit the St. Louis World's Fair. The world's fair showed inventions from around the world, and provided rides and food. Forty-five nations showed off their exhibits. One Missourian wrote, "When we first saw the Fair on Opening Day, April 30, 1904, with the flags catching the breeze and the sound of music everywhere, we suddenly discovered that we were all very proud. We admired everything: the statues, the buildings, the fountains—the good and the bad. We liked it all!"

Everyone especially liked the new food. Hot dogs appeared for the first time in the world. Thirsty fairgoers could have a taste of the latest drinks such as iced tea and Dr. Pepper. Children wanted to try the new "fairy floss" (now known as cotton candy). There's even a story about an ice-cream man who ran out of bowls and asked the waffle man next door for help. Someone rolled a waffle into a cone, put ice cream in it, and the first ice-cream cone was born.

HARD TIMES IN MISSOURI

Good times quickly melted away when fighting broke out between countries in Europe during World War I (1914–1918). In 1917, the United States joined the war. Eager to help their country, more than 140,000 Missourians fought in the war. Their general was born and raised in Laclede, Missouri. His name was John Pershing. In less than two years, Pershing put together an army of more than two million soldiers who helped bring an end to the war.

A few years after the war, factories started making more products than people could buy. They began losing money. Many had to close their doors, putting workers out of jobs. Prices for farm products went down, and the farmers had no money. These conditions led to a period of hard times called the Great Depression.

The depression, which began in 1929, affected the entire United States. The United States government tried to help by creating an organization called the Civilian Conservation Corps, or the CCC. The CCC offered jobs and training to unemployed people (people without jobs) across the United States. More than

CCC workers in Missouri created many public works, including roads and highways.

100,000 Missourians worked for the CCC building roads, parks, schools, wildlife habitats, and ponds.

The United States began to recover from the depression at the start of World War II (1939–1945). Once again, the war began in Europe, but this time Japan was also involved. The United States joined the war on December 8, 1941, after Japan bombed a United States naval base in Hawaii called Pearl Harbor.

From the Missouri River Valley to the Ozarks, more than 450,000 soldiers left their homes and jobs to serve their country. Leading the American soldiers in Europe was another man from Missouri, General Omar Bradley. At home, Missourians produced bomber airplanes, ships, and dynamite for the war. In all, they shipped more than $4 billion worth of supplies. The increased production provided jobs for many workers and helped end the depression for Missouri and the rest of the country.

Many women in Missouri took factory jobs during World War II, in place of men who had gone to war.

OMAR BRADLEY

WHO'S WHO IN MISSOURI?

General Omar Bradley (1893–1981) was born and raised in Clark, Missouri. He led 1.3 million American soldiers to victory in World War II. Because he cared so much about his men, he became the most popular general in the war, earning him the nickname "the Soldier's General."

THE RIGHTS OF ALL MISSOURIANS

After Missourians helped win World War II, Missouri grew into a strong manufacturing state with many jobs. Automobiles, airplanes, food products, and chemicals were some of the products coming from Missouri.

African-Americans were among the few people in Missouri who were not prospering. Although they had been freed from slavery almost one hundred years earlier, they were still not treated well by whites. They were still expected to eat in separate restaurants, use different public facilities, and attend different schools. This practice was called segregation. African-Americans demanded their rights and equal treatment.

In 1977, the Kansas City school system was taken to court for creating poor schools for African-American students. Most schools were still segregated. White schools were in better condition, and white children were doing better on test scores. St. Louis had the same problem. The court forced Missouri to desegregate, or end the separation, so everyone could get a quality education. Today, the Missouri school system is still trying to address school integration.

African-Americans protested segregation at the Board of Education in St. Louis in 1963.

A RIVER RISES

Missouri's recent history has focused in large part on its two large rivers—the Mississippi and the Missouri. Starting in May 1993, rain fell almost continuously in many parts of the Midwest, causing both rivers to rise over their banks and flood the land. It was one of the worst floods in our country's history. Missouri was hit the hardest, resulting in billions of dollars of damage. Bridges were knocked down, highways were closed, and buildings were flooded.

Even before the 1993 flood, the Missouri River Region Corps of Engineers kept close watch on the dams and bridges along the Missouri River. The Corps decides exactly how much water will flow through each dam.

Some Missourians are concerned about the decline of the Missouri River's environment and endangered species. Sometimes, the operation of dams affects fish reproduction and nesting wildlife. Some people want the river to flow naturally, without dams. Others, such as barge owners and fishermen, want the river to be managed because they use it to earn money. The Corps of Engineers is trying to find a solution that will be best for all Missourians.

Floodwaters overwhelmed Jefferson City during the Great Flood of 1993.

Missourians work hard to protect their environmental resources as they look ahead to the future. They want their citizens to have a good life and still keep their past alive. It's a tough challenge, but Missouri has shown through its history that it is a strong state.

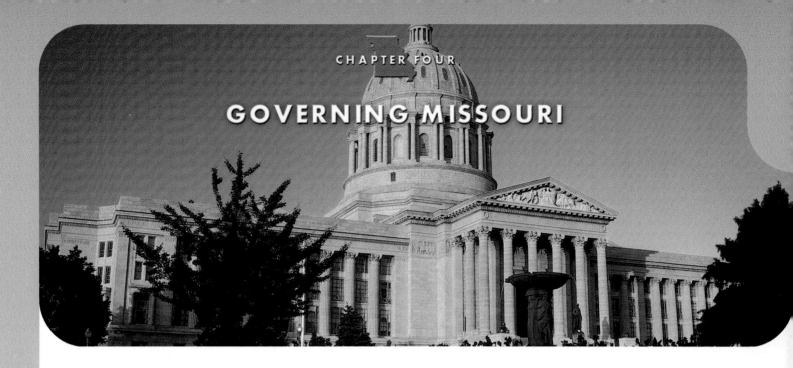

CHAPTER FOUR

GOVERNING MISSOURI

The Missouri constitution is a document outlining citizens' rights. Missouri's constitution describes rights such as freedom of religion and freedom of speech. The constitution also describes how the government works, including how the governor is chosen and who makes the laws.

The constitution that Missouri uses today was written in 1945. Other constitutions were written in 1820, 1865, and 1875, but they are no longer used. Without writing a new constitution, changes can be made by adding amendments. An amendment must be voted on and approved by the citizens in order to be added to the constitution.

Missouri's government has three parts, or branches, like the United States government: the executive, the legislative, and the judicial. The members of each branch work together to make sure that everyone in Missouri is healthy and prosperous.

The Missouri capitol, completed in 1918, houses the governor's office and the state legislative chambers.

The legislative branch makes the laws. *Legislative* means having the power to make laws. Missouri citizens over eighteen years of age have the right to help choose state legislators, the people who make laws. Missourians vote for two different groups of lawmakers: the house of representatives and the senate. Together they are called the General Assembly.

Within the walls of the state capitol, the General Assembly argues, discusses, and votes on new laws. The house of representatives meets in a room on one side of the building, and the senate meets in a room on the other side. Placing their rooms on opposite sides reminds everyone that each group has equal power.

The house of representatives has 163 members. Each member is called a representative. A representative is a person who speaks or acts for a large group of people. Each representative is a member for two years and may be elected for up to eight years. He or she must be at least twenty-four years old.

The Missouri General Assembly meets from January through mid-May to discuss new laws.

On the other side of a grand stairway is the door to the senate's chamber. Members of the senate are called senators. Each of Missouri's 34 senators must be at least thirty years old and is elected for four years.

When someone has an idea for a new law, it may be brought to the General Assembly in the form of a bill, which is a rough draft of the new law. There are bills for education, crime, health care, and taxes, among other things. For a bill to become a law in Missouri, it must be approved by the house of representatives and the senate. After both the house of representatives and the senate vote in favor of a law, it goes to the governor's office. If the governor approves, he or she signs it and the bill becomes law.

EXECUTIVE BRANCH

The executive branch makes sure Missouri's laws are enforced, or put into action. The governor is in charge of the executive branch. He or she is chosen by the people of Missouri and must be at least thirty years old. The governor is elected for four years. He or she is the state's chief law enforcement officer. His or her job also includes approving or rejecting bills from the General Assembly, and putting together a budget, which determines how the state's money will be spent. The governor is also in charge of the state's armed forces.

The lieutenant governor is also part of the executive branch. Elected by the people of Missouri, the lieutenant governor is president of the senate and takes the governor's place if he or she is away. Other departments in the executive branch handle issues related to agriculture (farming), education, and natural resources. The governor chooses, or appoints, people to be in charge of these departments.

The Missouri Supreme Court building, built in 1907, is open to the public for tours.

JUDICIAL BRANCH

Behind the capitol building stands a three-story red brick building. This is the office of the third branch of the Missouri government, the judicial branch. *Judicial* means having to do with courts and judges. Most Missourians obey the laws, however, some people break them. When a person has broken a law, he or she is taken to court.

Cases usually begin in circuit court. If a person does not like the final decision of the circuit court, he or she may ask a higher (more important) court, called the Court of Appeals, to hear the facts of the case again. The higher court then determines if the lower court's decision was correct. This is called an *appeal*.

The highest court in Missouri is the state supreme court, which makes final

MISSOURI STATE GOVERNMENT

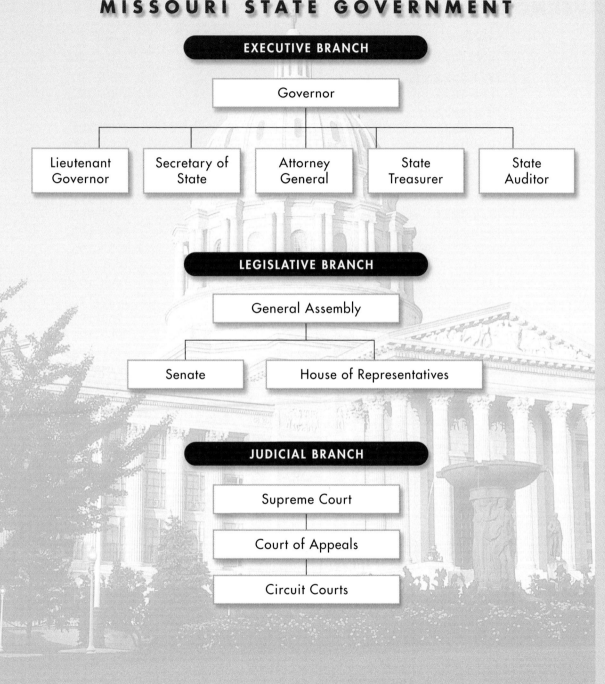

EXECUTIVE BRANCH

Governor

Lieutenant Governor | Secretary of State | Attorney General | State Treasurer | State Auditor

LEGISLATIVE BRANCH

General Assembly

Senate | House of Representatives

JUDICIAL BRANCH

Supreme Court

Court of Appeals

Circuit Courts

MISSOURI GOVERNORS

Name	Term	Name	Term
Alexander McNair	1820–1824	William Joel Stone	1893–1897
Frederick Bates	1824–1825	Lon Vest Stephens	1897–1901
Abraham J. Williams	1825–1826	Alexander Monroe Dockery	1901–1905
John Miller	1826–1832	Joseph Wingate Folk	1905–1909
Daniel Dunklin	1832–1836	Herbert Spencer Hadley	1909–1913
Lilburn W. Boggs	1836–1840	Elliott Woolfolk Major	1913–1917
Thomas Reynolds	1840–1844	Frederick Dozier Gardner	1917–1921
Meredith Miles Marmaduke	1844	Arthur Mastick Hyde	1921–1925
John Cummins Edwards	1844–1848	Sam Aaron Baker	1925–1929
Austin Augustus King	1848–1853	Henry Stewart Caulfield	1929–1933
Sterling Price	1853–1857	Guy Brasfield Park	1933–1937
Trusten Polk	1857	Lloyd Crow Stark	1937–1941
Hancock Lee Jackson	1857	Forrest C. Donnell	1941–1945
Robert Marcellus Stewart	1857–1861	Phil C. Donnelly	1945–1949
Claiborne Fox Jackson	1861	Forrest Smith	1949–1953
Hamilton Rowan Gamble	1861–1864	Phil M. Donnelly	1953–1957
Willard Preble Hall	1864–1865	James T. Blair Jr.	1957–1961
Thomas Clement Fletcher	1865–1869	John M. Dalton	1961–1965
Joseph Washington McClurg	1869–1871	Warren E. Hearnes	1965–1973
Benjamin Gratz Brown	1871–1873	Christopher S. Bond	1973–1977
Silas Woodson	1873–1875	Joseph P. Teasdale	1977–1981
Charles Henry Hardin	1875–1877	Christopher S. Bond	1981–1985
John Smith Phelps	1877–1881	John Ashcroft	1985–1993
Thomas Theodore Crittenden	1881–1885	Mel Carnahan	1993–2000
John Sappington Marmaduke	1885–1887	Roger B. Wilson	2000–2001
Albert Pickett Morehouse	1887–1889	Bob Holden	2001–
David Rowland Francis	1889–1893		

decisions about the meaning of Missouri's laws and constitution. The state supreme court is also in charge of all the courts in Missouri. Seven justices (judges) serve on the state supreme court, including one chief justice. The chief justice is head of the supreme court.

TAKE A TOUR OF THE STATE CAPITAL, JEFFERSON CITY

Jefferson City became the capital of Missouri in 1821. The city was built on the beautiful hills and valleys of the Missouri River in central Missouri. Today there are 39,636 people living in the capital city. It is not one of Missouri's largest cities, but it has many businesses and historical landmarks, such as the Missouri state capitol building.

Before the present capitol was built in 1917, there were two other capitol buildings in Jefferson City. The first burned down in 1837. On February 5, 1911, a bolt of

From the first floor rotunda, you can get a good view of the capitol dome, which includes murals and a bronze chandelier.

to Runge
Nature Center

to Washington
Park

WEST MAIN ST.

BROADWAY ST.

WEST HIGH ST.

WASHINGTON ST.

JEFFERSON ST.

MADISON ST.

MONROE ST.

EAST STATE ST.

E. CAPITOL AVE.

E. MILLER ST.

W. McCARTY ST.

State Capitol

All Missouri
Veterans
Memorial

Jefferson Landing
State Historic Site

Elizabeth
Rozier
Gallery

Governor's
Mansion

Cole County
Historical Museum/
Upschulte House

GOVERNOR'S
GARDEN

Missouri River

N

JEFFERSON CITY
Downtown

48

lightning struck the dome of Missouri's second capitol. The building exploded into flames and burned to the ground. The next day, Senator William Warner announced, "I have no tears to shed over the fact that the building has been destroyed . . . as it was not in keeping with the requirements of our great state."

The people of Missouri then built a new capitol made of pure white stone to show everyone how much their state government had grown. High on a bluff, the building overlooks the Missouri River. With enough space to fit thirty football fields, it is one hundred times larger than the state's first capitol. Its 13-foot- (4-m-) high giant bronze doors open to a stairway that is said to be the widest in the world. Outside, a bronze statue of Ceres, the Greek goddess of grain, stands on top of the building's dome and can be seen for miles.

Across the street from the capitol, lovely gardens and pathways lead to the governor's mansion. Guides dressed in old-fashioned clothing greet visitors and take them on a tour of the beautiful rooms where the governor and his family live.

EXTRA! EXTRA!

In 1935, Missouri artist Thomas Hart Benton was asked to paint a mural for the Missouri capitol building. A *mural* is a large painting on a wall. His painting, called *A Social History of Missouri*, covered all four walls in the House Lounge. It was not immediately liked because, although many Missourians thought it should portray state heroes, Benton's mural showed outlaws, slavery, and the Civil War. Over time, however, it became one of the best-liked and most famous paintings in America.

At Jefferson's Landing near the river, the dock looks the same as it did in the 1800s. It's easy to imagine a time when steamboats chugged up the Missouri River bringing pioneers, fur traders, and settlers. Across the street is another old building from the 1800s, the Union Hotel. It is now home to the Elizabeth Rozier Gallery, an art gallery that shows Missouri art.

Nearby is the Cole County Historical Museum. Built in 1871, this building now houses pieces of Missouri's history, such as Civil War uniforms and guns. There are also inaugural gowns worn by past governors' wives. (An *inaugural*, or *inauguration*, is a party welcoming a new governor.) Remember to visit Grandma's Attic on the third floor with its collection of antique toys.

Displays of Missouri's land and wildlife can be found a little farther west at the Runge Conservation Nature Center. After viewing the large aquarium full of Missouri fish, go outside and enjoy the scenery of Missouri while hiking on nature trails.

CHAPTER FIVE

THE PEOPLE AND PLACES OF MISSOURI

A **fiddler's music fills the room.** Square dancers step to the beat. With smiling faces, clapping hands, twirling skirts, and stomping boots, Missourians enjoy a good party. The fiddle is Missouri's state instrument, and the square dance is its state dance. Put the two together, and the people of Missouri know how to celebrate.

According to the 2000 census, Missouri has more than five million people—5,595,211 to be exact. Missourians come from all over the world. Some families are descended from African-Americans who were brought there hundreds of years ago. Some are the great-great-great grandchildren of settlers from Ireland, Germany, Norway, Italy, Mexico, and dozens of other countries. Some simply moved to Missouri from faraway places such as the Middle East.

To get an idea of how many people come from each place, imagine one hundred square dancers dancing in a circle. Eighty-five dancers

Missourians of German heritage celebrate with a traditional dance.

would be from countries in Europe. Eleven would be African-American and two would be Hispanic (from a Spanish-speaking country, such as Mexico). The final two would be from other countries.

Many of the first settlers who came to Missouri were hunters and farmers who lived off the land. When factories opened in the cities, some farmers moved there to find work and make more money. Today, 3 million people live in Missouri's cities, mostly in St. Louis and Kansas City.

Missouri is ranked tenth in total corn production in the United States.

WORKING IN MISSOURI

The first pioneers and settlers in Missouri worked hard to settle the land. Today Missourians work in many different kinds of jobs, such as mining lead, assembling automobiles, and raising cattle.

In Missouri, there are 109,000 farms, the second highest amount in the nation. For every one hundred farms in the country, five are in Missouri. Most of these farms are about 265 acres (107 hectares) in size. Altogether, farmers work about 29 million acres (11,745,000 ha) of land in Missouri—about the size of Pennsylvania. Missouri farmers say they work from "can see to can't see," which means long days in the field from daylight to darkness.

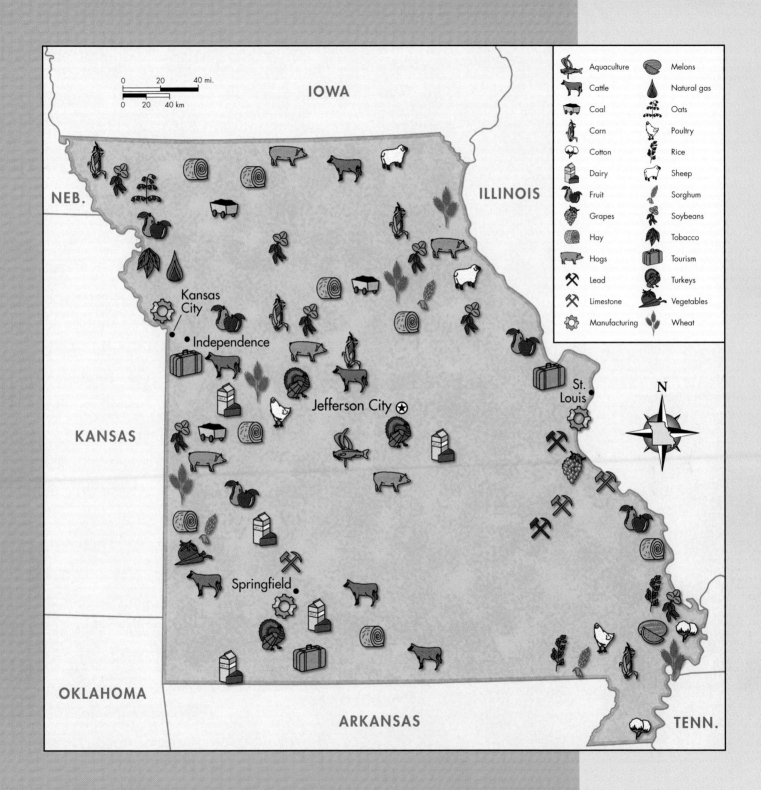

IOWA

NEB.

ILLINOIS

KANSAS

OKLAHOMA

ARKANSAS

TENN.

Kansas City

Independence

Jefferson City

St. Louis

Springfield

0   20   40 mi.
0   20   40 km

N

Aquaculture	Melons
Cattle	Natural gas
Coal	Oats
Corn	Poultry
Cotton	Rice
Dairy	Sheep
Fruit	Sorghum
Grapes	Soybeans
Hay	Tobacco
Hogs	Tourism
Lead	Turkeys
Limestone	Vegetables
Manufacturing	Wheat

The most popular crops in Missouri are soybeans and corn, grown mostly in northern and southeastern Missouri. Hay is the third most popular crop and is grown all over the state, but especially in the south central and southwestern areas. Farmers in the boot heel grow cotton and rice.

Farms are not just for growing crops. Raising animals is also an important part of Missouri farming. Missouri's production of beef cattle is second in the country. Missourians raise beef cattle in the central, south central, and southwestern areas of the state. They raise hogs in the north central and west central areas of Missouri. Missourians also raise turkeys and chickens, grow watermelons, and even make wine.

Meanwhile, more than 400,000 Missourians are busy working in one of Missouri's 10,000 manufacturing companies. At Hallmark Cards' International Headquarters in Kansas City, people make invitations and greeting cards that are sent all over the world. At the Boeing Company in St. Louis, engineers build fighter jets for the United States armed forces. Vehi-

Mechanics work on a military helicopter in St. Louis.

cles are manufactured in Kansas City and St. Louis, including motorcycles, vans, and cars.

Many of these vehicles travel on roads made of cement that comes from Missouri. Cement is made from crushed stones mined in 138 quarries across Missouri. Missouri miners have a saying, "If it can't be grown, it has to be mined." Missouri has more than 5,000 miners and produces the majority of lead mined in the United States. Each year, $1 billion of lead, zinc, copper, and silver is mined in Missouri.

Digging up these metals can destroy the land, however. Missouri's miners work hard to keep the land in use after they are finished mining. According to the Mining Industry Council of Missouri, "Many of the

A tourist peers out at the city from the top of the Gateway Arch.

public lands being mined today will become the wildlife refuges, recreation parks and housing or business developments of tomorrow."

A big business in Missouri is tourism. Tourism is the business of providing food, entertainment, and shelter for people who are traveling. The beauty of Missouri's Ozark region makes it one of the country's favorite vacation spots. In one year, tourists spent $8 billion in Missouri, mostly to visit sites in the Ozarks, St. Louis, and Kansas City.

When tourists travel on vacation, many people are needed to take care of the travelers. Hotels, restaurants, shops, and parks are some of the places that have workers to serve people. These kinds of jobs are part of the service industry. The service industry is the largest in Missouri. More than half of all Missourians work in the service industry.

TAKE A TOUR OF MISSOURI

Northwestern Missouri

Someone once said, "They planted Kansas City and the darn thing grew." What started out as a trading post and a small river town has blossomed into Missouri's largest city and one of the most beautiful in the world.

With bubbling fountains, interesting statues, and colorful murals, the Kansas City Country Club Plaza is the country's oldest shopping mall, built in 1920. Today there are more than two hundred shops and restaurants in the plaza. All the artwork and sculptures make up an outdoor museum worth more than $1 million.

Thanks to its many fountains, Kansas City has earned the nickname "City of Fountains."

Adding to the beauty of Kansas City is the Kansas City Symphony, with musicians from around the world performing classical music. A symphony is a large group of people with different instruments who play music together. Kansas City has other musical groups for local musicians. One of those is the Youth Symphony of Kansas City. Children have been performing with this orchestra for 42 years.

For sports fans, Kansas City is home to the Harry S. Truman Sports Complex. Both the Kansas City Royals baseball team and the Kansas City Chiefs football team call the sports complex home. Completed in 1973, it is the only place in the country with side-by-side football and baseball stadiums.

Nearby, in Independence, is the Truman Presidential Museum and Library. The library preserves the papers, records, and other historical materials of President Harry S. Truman. You can find out more about his life and career by exploring the memorabilia on display at the museum.

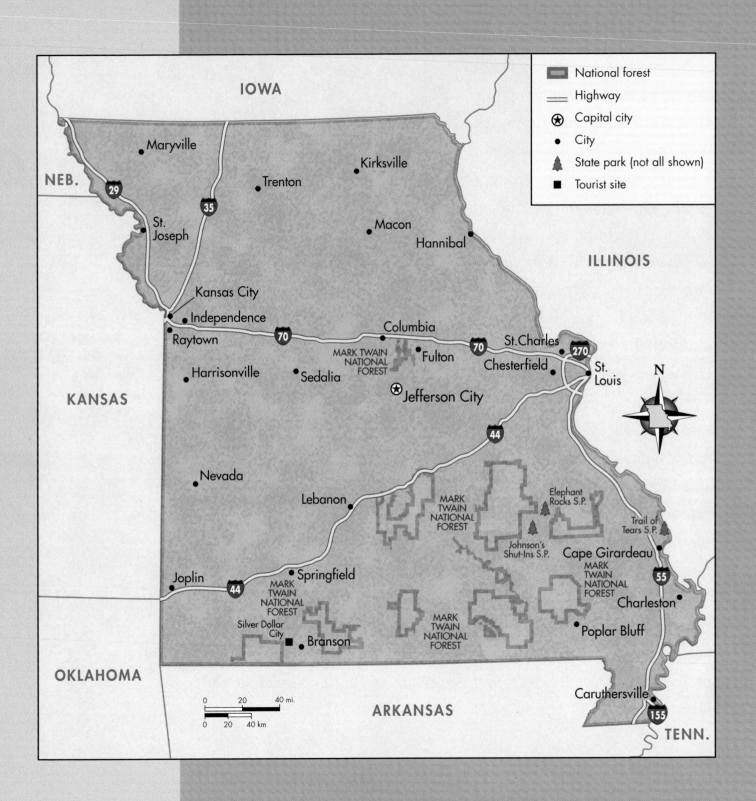

IOWA

NEB.

29

Maryville

Trenton

Kirksville

St.
Joseph

35

Macon

Hannibal

ILLINOIS

Kansas City

Independence

Raytown

70

Columbia

Fulton

MARK TWAIN
NATIONAL
FOREST

70

St. Charles

270

Chesterfield

St.
Louis

KANSAS

Harrisonville

Sedalia

⊛ Jefferson City

44

N

Nevada

Lebanon

MARK
TWAIN
NATIONAL
FOREST

Elephant
Rocks S.P. 🌲

Trail of
Tears S.P. 🌲

🌲

Johnson's
Shut-Ins S.P.

Cape Girardeau

55

MARK
TWAIN
NATIONAL
FOREST

Joplin

44

Springfield

MARK
TWAIN
NATIONAL
FOREST

MARK
TWAIN
NATIONAL
FOREST

Charleston

Poplar Bluff

Silver Dollar
City ■ Branson

OKLAHOMA

0   20   40 mi.

0   20   40 km

ARKANSAS

Caruthersville

155

TENN.

Legend:
- National forest
- Highway
- ⊛ Capital city
- • City
- 🌲 State park (not all shown)
- ■ Tourist site

Every April 3, visitors gather in St. Joseph to compete in the Pony Express race. Running through an obstacle course, children race to get the mail delivered just like Pony Express riders did in 1860. This race celebrates the first time a Pony Express rider left St. Joseph to deliver mail to California. At that time, it took one month for a letter to go across the country, but it took just ten days for the Pony Express to deliver mail between St. Joseph and Sacramento. Within two years, the telegraph (a way to communicate with code over wires) replaced the Pony Express. Because it was a great example of "American creativity and ambition," the Pony Express has become a legend in history.

One of Missouri's most famous outlaws died in St. Joseph. His name was Jesse James. Some people liked him because when he robbed a bank he ripped up bank records that said who owed the bank money. In 1882, Jesse was shot and killed for reward money in his own home, which has since been turned into a museum with personal items and photographs of Jesse and his family on display.

Northeastern Missouri

In Hannibal, the fourth of July is time to celebrate the national Tom Sawyer Days Festival. *The Adventures of Tom Sawyer* is a book written by Missouri's most famous resident, Samuel Clemens, also known as Mark

EXTRA! EXTRA!

Jesse James, along with other outlaws, got his start during the Civil War. In Missouri, the war was not fought just between soldiers. There were also two groups of vicious fighters. The Jayhawkers fought against slavery supporters, and the Bushwhackers—including Jesse James—were loyal to the Confederacy. Bushwhackers were known to be violent, destroying towns, killing people, and robbing banks. Once the war ended, some Bushwackers continued to terrorize the western frontier.

Twain. When he wrote about growing up in Hannibal, Twain used his real-life adventures. Some of these adventures are celebrated during the festival, like the fence-painting and frog-jumping contests. Bring your own frog or rent one for a dollar at the rent-a-frog booth.

Farther south is St. Louis, Missouri's second largest city and home to many famous companies, such as Anheuser-Busch, the world's largest beer brewer. A tour of the St. Louis brewery includes a brew house,

A boy encourages his frog at a frog jumping contest.

WHO'S WHO IN MISSOURI?

Samuel Clemens (1835–1910) was born in Florida, Missouri, and moved to Hannibal as a young boy. Before he became a writer, he worked as a printer and a riverboat pilot on the Mississippi River. Using the name Mark Twain, he wrote books about growing up on the Mississippi. Among his best-known books are *The Adventures of Tom Sawyer* and *The Adventures of Huckleberry Finn*.

where the beer is made, and the lager cellar, where the beer is stored. (Lager is another word for beer.) There is also a packaging plant where beer is poured into bottles and cans to be shipped out. The tour even includes the Clydesdale stables, where Anheuser-Busch's world famous Clydesdale horses are kept.

Another stop in St. Louis is the famous Gateway Arch. Built in 1965 and designed by Eero Saarinen, the Arch honors Missouri's history. Towering over the land, it is a symbol of Missouri's role as the "Gateway to the West." Climb aboard a specially designed tram system and ride 630 feet (192 m) up for a view that stretches 30 miles

Seventy-five feet (23 m) taller than the Washington Monument, the Gateway Arch is the tallest monument in the United States.

(48 km). The arch is as tall as a 63-story building. On a windy day, the Arch sways back and forth, up to 1 inch (2.54 cm).

If you keep your eyes to the sky, you might catch one of St. Louis' special events. Around the beginning of football season, high in the clouds, racers in the Great Forest Park's Hot Air Balloon Race rise above St. Louis. As the ballooners glide along, they enjoy a beautiful view of Missouri's trees. At this time of year, leaves change from green to blazing yellow, orange, and red.

Back on the ground, nothing matches the crack of the bat and the roar of the crowd when St. Louis residents cheer for their hometown baseball team, the St. Louis Cardinals, in Busch Stadium. They also cheer for their

Busch Stadium seats almost 50,000 baseball fans.

The USS *Missouri* was a famous battleship used in World War II. When President Truman visited the battleship, the cook, Chief Steward Harry Hightower, made this pie for his visit. However, Hightower refused to give out the recipe when the president asked for it! When Hightower retired in 1970, he shared this recipe for President Truman's favorite pie. Don't forget to ask an adult for help!

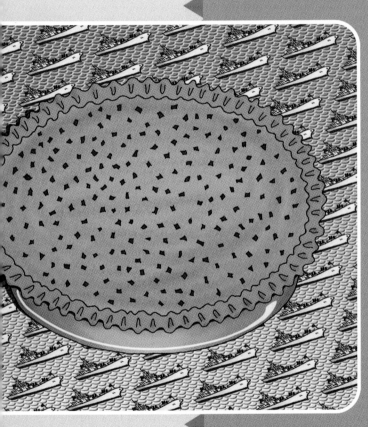

USS *MISSOURI* BUTTERMILK PIE

(makes 8 servings)

Ingredients:
2 cups granulated sugar
1/4 cup (1 stick) butter, softened
3 eggs
3 tablespoons flour
1/4 teaspoon salt
1 cup buttermilk
1 9-inch ready-made pie crust
1/2 cup chopped pecans, toasted

1. Preheat oven to 300° F. In large mixing bowl, slowly beat sugar into butter with an electric mixer until well blended.
2. Beat in eggs, one at a time.
3. Mix in flour and salt.
4. Beat in buttermilk until mixture is well blended. Pour filling into crust.
5. Sprinkle toasted pecans over filling.
6. Bake for 1 hour and 15 minutes, or until filling is set. Let cool. Store pie in refrigerator.

Note: To toast chopped pecans, spread evenly in shallow baking pan. Bake in 350° F oven for 5–10 minutes or until browned, stirring once or twice during baking.

football team, the St. Louis Rams, and their professional hockey team, the St. Louis Blues. Sports are big in St. Louis, and the city doesn't miss a chance to celebrate.

Southeastern Missouri

Heading southeast, stop at Trail of Tears State Park in Cape Girardeau County. The park is dedicated to an eastern Native American tribe, the Cherokee. In 1838, the Cherokee were forced to leave the southeastern United States and walk 1,000 miles (1,609 km) west to Oklahoma, because the American government drove them from their land. On their sad journey, called the Trail of Tears, they passed through Missouri, where the park is today. A visitor's center has information about the Native Americans' walk. A decorative wooden building stands in the park as a memorial to the Native Americans. It is named the Otahki Memorial, after a Cherokee princess who died along the trail.

Not far from Cape Girardeau, near Graniteville, follow a trail that leads through a maze of monstrous granite boulders that stand "end to end like a train of circus elephants." These one-billion-year-old boulders started out as cracks in the rock. Over millions of years, water and wind wore away at the cracks. Eventually the cracks became so big that separate boulders were made. Most of the boulders at Elephant Rocks State Park are found in the 7-acre (3-ha) Elephant Rocks Natural Area. There is a picnic area near the rocks, and they are fun to climb if you can!

You can explore a maze of giant red granite rocks at Elephant Rocks State Park.

Close by are the Johnson's Shut-Ins. For thousands of years, rivers wore away at the rock and created gorges. A gorge is a deep and narrow valley that usually has very steep and rocky sides, with a river at the bottom. These gorges are part of Johnson's Shut-Ins State Park, a popular place for rogainers. Rogaining is the sport of long-distance, 24-hour races. Teams travel entirely on foot and may only use a compass and a map to follow a rugged path through the gorges.

Missouri's only national forest is the Mark Twain National Forest. These beautiful woodlands cover 1.5 million acres (607,500 ha) of land in southern and central Missouri. There are fourteen streams to float on, sixteen lakes for water sports, and trails for hiking, biking, and horseback riding.

Southwestern Missouri

Some of the biggest celebrations in Missouri happen during winter in the Ozark Mountains. Silver Dollar City is decked out in Christmas decorations, celebrating the season with An Old Time Christmas festival that goes on for two months.

Missouri's third largest city, Springfield, is also set in the rolling hills of southwest Missouri. Visit the Springfield Art Museum, or check out the Discovery Center for hands-on learning. You can also tour a cave at Fantastic Caverns, or visit the world-famous Bass Pro Shops Outdoor World. Known as the "granddaddy of outdoor stores," the Bass Pro Shops Outdoor World has something for everyone. A giant aquarium with daily shows, a pretend forest with pretend campfires, a 30-foot (9-m) waterfall, turtle ponds, and two restaurants are some of the things found in this amazing store.

Branson, in the Ozarks, has more than forty music theaters lining the streets. Talented musicians from all over the world perform in the area's 11,000 shows each year, including country music, rock, ragtime,

Giant sculptures of John Wayne, Elvis Presley, Marilyn Monroe, and Charlie Chaplin adorn the front of the Hollywood Wax Museum in Branson.

and even comedy and magic shows. Other famous stars can be seen at the Hollywood Wax Museum—as life-size wax figures, of course! You can get a glimpse of famous presidents in the Hall of Presidents, or tip-toe through the crypt, where figures of scary creatures such as Dracula are lurking in the dark. The figures of television, movie, and music stars will take you on a journey through entertainment history.

Wrap up in a handmade quilt from Branson's annual Heart of the Ozarks Arts and Crafts Festival. Artists from the area come to show off their crafts. Skills in quilting, woodworking, doll making, and basket weaving are handed down from Missouri mothers to daughters, and fathers to sons.

Settlers and pioneers came with dreams and hopes of building a home where "the welfare of the people shall be the supreme law." This is Missouri's state motto. Brave pioneers dreamed of a land that would give them the chance to find happiness, health, and prosperity. Missouri has helped make many of these settlers' dreams come true.

MISSOURI ALMANAC

Statehood date and number: August 10, 1821/24th state

State seal: The Missouri seal begins with a group of 23 small stars and one large star, because Missouri was the 24th state. Underneath, there are two grizzly bears holding a belt bearing the words "United we stand, divided we fall." Within the belt is the symbol for the United States (the bald eagle), a silver crescent moon, and a bear. The grizzly bears stand on a scroll with the state motto in Latin. Adopted on January 11, 1822.

State flag: The flag has three horizontal stripes of red, white, and blue. The state seal is in the center of the flag, surrounded by 24 stars. Adopted March 22, 1913.

Geographic center: Miller County, 20 miles (32 km) southwest of Jefferson City

Total area/rank: 69,709 square miles (180,545 sq km)/21st

Borders: Iowa, Arkansas, Nebraska, Kansas, Oklahoma, Illinois, Kentucky, and Tennessee

Latitude and longitude: Missouri is located approximately between 36° and 40° 35' N and 85° 5' and 95° 45' W.

Highest/lowest elevation: Taum Sauk Mountain in the St. Francois Mountains, 1,772 feet (540 m)/St. Francois River at the Arkansas border, 230 feet (70 m)

Hottest/coldest temperature: 118° F (48° C) at Clinton on July 15, 1936/–40° F (–40° C) at Warsaw on February 13, 1905

Land area/rank: 68,896 square miles (178,441 sq km)/18th

Inland water area/rank: 811 square miles (2,100 sq km)/26th

Population/rank: 5,595,211 (2000 census)/17th

Population of major cities:
   Kansas City: 441,545
   St. Louis: 348,189
   Springfield: 151,580
   Independence: 113,288
   Columbia: 84,531
   St. Joseph: 73,990

Origin of state name: Fox Native American word meaning "big canoe people"

State capital: Jefferson City

Previous capitals: St. Louis, 1820; St. Charles, 1821–1826

Counties: 114

State government: 34 senators, 163 representatives

Major rivers/lakes:

Mississippi, Missouri, Osage, Meramec, Current, Grand Chariton, Gasconade, White, Salt, and St. Francis rivers/Harry S. Truman Reservoir, Lake of the Ozarks, Table Rock Lake, Mark Twain Lake, Lake Taneycomo, Bull Shoals Lake, Norfolk Lake, and Pomme de Terre

Farm products: Corn, wheat, cotton, soybeans, apples, watermelons, and dairy products

Livestock: Beef cattle, dairy cattle, hogs, chickens, turkeys, sheep, and mules

Manufactured products: Aircraft, automobiles, chemical products, food products, beer, machinery, electrical equipment, meat, flour, and medicines

Mining products: Lead, cobalt, limestone, marble, red granite, silica sand, fireclay, coal, and copper

Fishing products: Sport and game fish such as catfish, trout, bass, baitfish for fishing, fish for aquariums

Animal: Missouri mule

Bird: Bluebird

Fish: Channel catfish

Floral Emblem: White Hawthorn blossom

Folk dance: Square dance

Fossil: Crinoid

Insect: Honey bee

Mineral: Galena

Motto: Salus populi suprema lex esto. (Latin) "Let the welfare of the people be the supreme law."

Musical instrument: Fiddle

Nicknames: The Show Me State, Mother of the West, Gateway to the West, Home of the Blues

Rock: Mozarkite

Song: "Missouri Waltz," adopted June 30, 1949. Lyrics by James Royce Shannon; music by John Valentine Eppel

Tree: Flowering dogwood

Tree nut: Black walnut

Wildlife: Whitetail deer, coyotes, rabbits, opossums, skunks, raccoons, muskrats, red foxes, fox squirrels,

beavers, rattlesnakes, copperhead snakes, robins, blue jays, cardinals, owls, hawks, quail, geese, wild turkeys, meadow larks, bass, crappies, walleye, pike, trout, sturgeon, channel catfish

TIMELINE

MISSOURI STATE HISTORY

The first issue of the *Missouri Gazette* is published

René Auguste Chouteau cuts down trees for fur-trading post that later becomes St. Louis

The first steamboat, the *Independence*, chugs up the Missouri River

Bluff Dwellers live in caves along the river valley

Ceremony in St. Louis honoring the Louisiana Purchase gives the U.S. control of the Mississippi River

Gaslights light up St. Louis streets, and telegraph wires connect the city to the East Coast

Sieur de La Salle travels down the Mississippi and claims land for France

The country's strongest earthquake shakes the New Madrid area

10,000 years ago | 1682 | 1764 | 1804 | 1808 | 1811 | 1819 | 1847

1607 | 1620 | 1776 | 1783 | 1787 | 1812–15 | 1843

The first permanent British settlement at Jamestown, Virginia

American Revolutionary War ends

Pioneers travel West on the Oregon Trail

Pilgrims set up Plymouth colony

U.S. Constitution is written

American colonies declare independence from England

U.S. and England fight the War of 1812

UNITED STATES HISTORY

The Flood of the
Century causes
$3 billion of damage
in Missouri

The Kansas City
Royals beat the St.
Louis Cardinals in
the first all-Missouri
World Series, nick-
named the "I-70
Series"

Aunt Jemima's ready-mix pan-
cakes from St. Joseph are avail-
able for the first time

The first cross-state
railroad connects
Hannibal and St.
Joseph

The first Missouri television station, KSD-TV,
begins to broadcast

Missouri
Governor Mel
Carnahan dies
in a plane crash
with his son

The first U.S.
Olympics takes place
in St. Louis

1859   1889   1904   1947   1985   1993   2000

1846–48   1861–65   1917–18   1929   1941–45   1950–53   1964   1965–73   1969   1991   1995

U.S. takes part
in World War I

U.S. fights in
World War II

Civil rights laws
passed in the U.S.

U.S. and other nations
fight in Persian Gulf War

U.S. fights
war with
Mexico

The stock market
crashes and U.S.
enters the Great
Depression

U.S. fights in the
Vietnam War

Civil War
occurs in the
United States

U.S. fights in the
Korean War

Neil Armstrong
and Edwin
Aldrin land on
the moon

U.S. space shuttle
docks with Russian
space station

GALLERY OF FAMOUS MISSOURIANS

Josephine Baker
(1906–1975)
Famous dancer and singer. Her wild dances made her famous in Paris, France. In the United States in the 1950s and 1960s, she worked for the civil rights of African-Americans. Born in St. Louis.

Susan Elizabeth Blow
(1843–1916)
Established the first successful public kindergarten in the United States. It opened in 1873 in St. Louis. Born in St. Louis.

George Washington Carver
(1864–1943)
Scientist who encouraged farmers to plant different crops, such as peanuts, sweet potatoes, and soybeans, to help the soil become richer. He discovered many ways to use peanuts, including peanut butter. Born in Diamond Grove.

Scott Joplin
(1868–1917)
Music composer who became known as the "Father of Ragtime." (Ragtime is a type of piano music.) Lived in Sedalia and St. Louis.

Amanda "Ardelia" Hardin Palmer
(1875–1968)
Schoolteacher and community leader. In 1930 at the age of 55, she attended the United States Aircraft Engineering School in Kansas City and became the only woman aircraft instructor in the United States. Born in Jackson County.

James Cash Penney
(1875–1971)
Grew up to become a storekeeper. In 1904, he opened his first store, the J. C. Penney Company. By 1924, he had 500 stores across the country. Born in Hamilton.

Charles "Casey" Stengel
(1890–1975)
Professional baseball player. Throughout his career, he played for Brooklyn, Philadelphia, and New York. In 1966, he was elected to the National Baseball Hall of Fame. Born in Kansas City.

Harold Bell Wright
(1872–1944)
Author of *The Shepherd of the Hills*, a book about the people of the Ozarks. As a result, millions of people came to Branson to see where the story happened. This started the tourist business in the Ozarks.

GLOSSARY

admit: to let someone into a place

ancestor: relative who lived a long time ago

branch: a separate department or office that is part of a large group

classical: music written before the late 1800s

compromise: to settle a dispute by each side giving up something that it wants

confederacy: a union of states or peoples for a particular purpose

court: a place where a disagreement is decided by a judge and/or jury

import: to bring in from another country for sale or use

inhabit: to live in

manufacture: to make something in large numbers

prairie: a large piece of land with low rolling hills, grass, and few trees

ragtime: lively style of piano music derived from African-American folk music

region: part of the country

representative: a person who speaks or does something on behalf of a group of people

requirement: something that is needed or demanded

tax: monetary charge on a person's income or property

treaty: a formal, signed agreement between two parties

FOR MORE INFORMATION

Web sites

State of Missouri
http://www.state.mo.us/
Official web site of the Missouri government.

Bluff Dwellers Cave Virtual Tour
http://www.4noel.com/bluffd/bluffd2.htm
Take a tour of a famous cave in Missouri.

The Official Web Site of the Osage Nation
http://www.osagetribe.com
History of the tribe and information about the Osage today.

Books

Blackwood, Gary L. *Life on the Oregon Trail.* San Diego, CA: Lucent Books, 1999.

Doherty, Craig A. and Katherine M. *The Gateway Arch.* Woodbridge, CT: Blackbirch Press, 1995.

Lasky, Kathryn. *A Brilliant Streak: The Making of Mark Twain.* New York, NY: Harcourt Brace, 1998.

Schuman, Michael A. *Harry S. Truman.* Springfield, NJ: Enslow, 1997.

Addresses

Missouri Chamber of Commerce
428 E. Capitol Avenue
Jefferson City, MO 65102

State Historical Society of Missouri
1020 Lowry Street
Columbia, MO 65201-7298

Missouri Governor
Missouri Capitol Building, Room 218
P. O. Box 720
Jefferson City, MO 65102-0720

INDEX

ABOUT THE AUTHOR

Mary Ellen Lago works at The Writers Factory. She has completed two children's books and has written for an award-winning national magazine. She earned her bachelor of science degree from the University of Iowa in 1987. Mary Ellen lives in Clearwater, Florida, with her husband, Tony, and children, Trey, Diego, and Eva.